The Hole Truth! Underground Animal Life

Prairie Dog's Hideaway

by Dee Phillips

Consultants:

Suzy Gazlay, MA
Recipient, Presidential Award for Excellence in Science Teaching

Leah Birmingham, RVT
Assistant Director, Sandy Pines Wildlife Centre, Napanee, Ontario, Canada

Kimberly Brenneman, PhD
National Institute for Early Education Research, Rutgers University, New Brunswick, New Jersey

BEARPORT
PUBLISHING

NEW YORK, NEW YORK

Credits

Cover, © Henk Bentiage/Shutterstock; 4, © Jaana Piira/Shutterstock; 5, © Jim Brandenburg/Minden Pictures/FLPA; 6T, © Cosmographics; 6B, © Jim Brandenburg/Minden Pictures/FLPA; 7, © Henk Bentiage/Shutterstock; 8, © Joe Ferrer/Shutterstock; 9, © Flirt/Superstock; 10, ©, lightpoet/Shutterstock; II, © Ruby Tuesday Books Ltd.; I2TL, © Roberta Olenick/All Canada Photos/Superstock; I2TR, © Creativex/Shutterstock; I2BL, © visceralimage/Shutterstock; I2BR, © Stephen Mcsweeny/Shutterstock; 13, © Marka/Superstock; 14, © Jim Brandenburg/Minden Pictures/FLPA; I5, © Don Johnston/All Canada Photos/Superstock; 16, © Karel Gallas/Shutterstock; 17, © Don Johnston/All Canada Photos/Superstock; 18, © W. Perry Conway/Corbis; 19, © W. Perry Conway/Corbis; 20, © Henk Bentiage/Shutterstock; 2I, © Henk Bentiage/Shutterstock; 22, © Eric Isselée/Shutterstock; 23TL, © Jaana Piira/Shutterstock; 23TC, © Cheryl Ann Quigley/Shutterstock; 23TR, © Jim Brandenburg/Minden Pictures/FLPA; 23BL, © Michal Ninger/Shutterstock; 23BC, © Brian Lasenby/Shutterstock; 23BR, © Jim Brandenburg/Minden Pictures/FLPA.

Publisher: Kenn Goin
Senior Editor: Lisa Wiseman
Creative Director: Spencer Brinker
Design: Alix Wood
Editor: Mark J. Sachner
Photo Researcher: Ruby Tuesday Books Ltd

Library of Congress Cataloging in Publication Data

Phillips, Dee, 1967–
  Prairie dog's hideaway / by Dee Phillips.
      p. cm. — (The hole truth!: Underground animal life)
  Includes bibliographical references and index.
  ISBN 978 1 61772 408 4 (library binding) — ISBN 1 61772 408 4 (library binding)
 I. Prairie dogs—Behavior Juvenile literature. 2. Prairie dogs—Habitations—Juvenile literature.
I. Title.
  QL737.R68P454 2012
  599.36'7—dc23

                        2011045195

For more information, write to Bearport Publishing Company, Inc., 45 West 2lst Street, Suite 3B, New York, New York I00I0. Printed in the United States of America.

I0 9 8 7 6 5 4 3

Contents

A Prairie Dog Town

It is early morning in a little town.

There are no houses, though—just small mounds of dirt.

Suddenly, a prairie dog pops its head out of a hole in one of the mounds.

The hole is the entrance to the little animal's underground home.

prairie dog

prairie dog town

Prairie dogs dig underground homes, in which they sleep, raise their babies, and stay safe from enemies.

prairie dog

mound

Check Out a Prairie Dog!

Prairie dogs are a type of **squirrel**.

There are five kinds of prairie dogs.

Black-tailed prairie dogs are the most common kind.

They dig their underground towns on open, grassy lands called **prairies**.

North America

Pacific Ocean

Atlantic Ocean

N W E S

Where black-tailed prairie dogs live

prairie

An adult black-tailed prairie dog is about 14 inches (36 cm) long. It weighs about two pounds (907 g).

black-tailed prairie dog

Imagine you are talking to a friend who has never seen a prairie dog. Describe what the animal looks like.

Prairie Dog Families

Prairie dogs live in small families.

A family usually has some adult females, their babies, and one adult male.

Just like in a human town, each family lives in its own small area, or **territory**.

The family digs its home, which is called a **burrow**, in its territory.

All the adults help build the burrow.

a prairie dog digging a burrow

Try to imagine what the inside of a prairie dog's burrow looks like. What type of rooms do you think the family will need in its underground home?

8

A prairie dog town is made up of many burrows. A different prairie dog family lives in each one.

Look Inside a Burrow

A prairie dog's burrow may have several entrances.

The entrances are connected to long tunnels.

Just below the entrance to one tunnel is a listening room.

Prairie dogs go into this room and listen for danger before going outside.

Farther down the tunnel there is a bedroom, where the family sleeps.

There may also be nesting rooms, where the females give birth.

mound

A prairie dog makes a mound of dirt around each entrance hole to its burrow. The mound keeps water from flowing into the burrow when it rains.

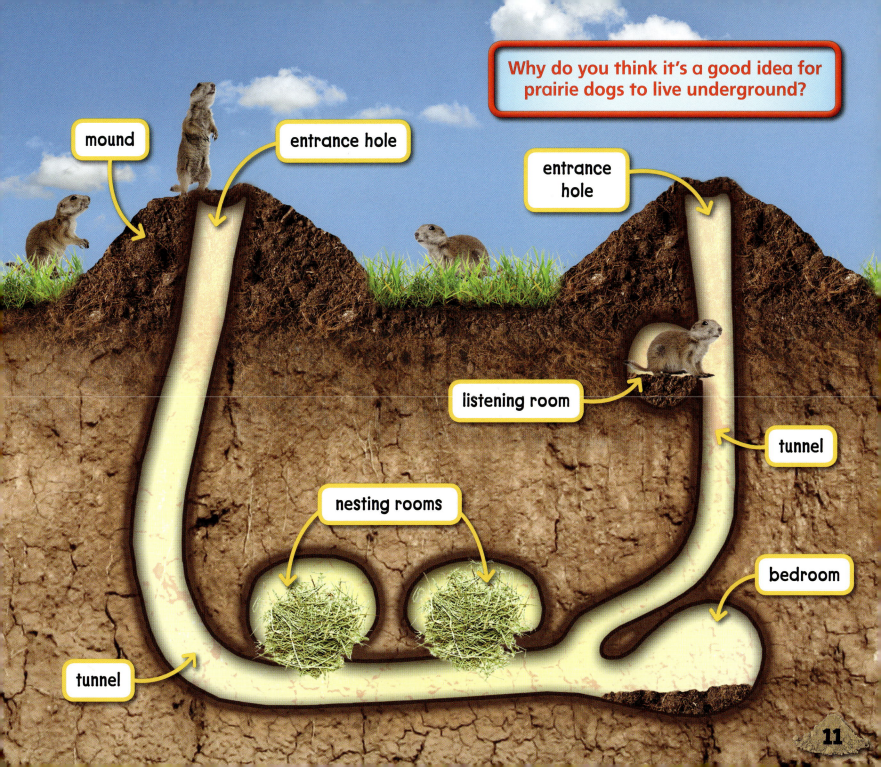

mound

entrance hole

entrance hole

Why do you think it's a good idea for prairie dogs to live underground?

listening room

tunnel

nesting rooms

tunnel

bedroom

11

A Quick Escape

Many animals hunt prairie dogs for food.

An underground home is a good place to hide from these **predators**.

Prairie dogs are in danger when they leave their burrows, though.

Whenever a predator is near, the prairie dogs dive underground.

Birds and larger enemies, such as coyotes, cannot follow the little animals into their homes.

Prairie Dog Predators

black-footed ferret

coyote

hawk

badger

What do you think this prairie dog is watching for?

Many animals eat prairie dogs, including coyotes, bobcats, badgers, snakes, falcons, hawks, black-footed ferrets, and eagles.

13

Watch Out! Danger!

When prairie dogs are above ground, they take turns looking out for predators.

If a prairie dog spots danger, it makes a "chirk, chirk" sound.

When its family and neighbors hear this sound, they quickly dive into their burrows.

The prairie dog looking out for predators makes a "wee oooh" noise once the danger is gone.

a prairie dog making a "chirk, chirk" noise

The "wee oooh" noise is also called a jump-yip. As the prairie dog makes the noise, it holds its front paws up in the air and jumps!

a prairie dog doing a jump-yip

15

A Prairie Dog's Day

As the sun comes up, prairie dogs leave their burrows.

They spend the day outside, looking for grass and small plants to eat.

If the weather is very hot, they may go back underground to cool off.

In winter, they return to the burrow to warm up on cold days.

Prairie dogs use their teeth to cut down tall grasses near their burrows. They do this so they can see predators coming near their town.

This female prairie dog is carrying grass to her burrow. What do you think she will use the grass for?

Prairie Dog Babies

Spring is the time of year when prairie dogs **mate**.

After mating, a female prairie dog digs a nesting room in her burrow.

She takes mouthfuls of dry grass into the room to make a nest.

Soon, she gives birth to three or four babies that need lots of care.

At first, the babies' eyes are closed and they cannot see.

The mother prairie dog feeds them milk from her body.

one-week-old prairie dogs

A newborn prairie dog is about three inches (7.6 cm) long. It weighs the same as three quarters.

a three-week-old prairie dog

19

Leaving the Burrow

After five weeks, the baby prairie dogs have grown fur and their eyes are open.

At six weeks old, they can leave their burrow for the first time.

Outside, the babies play with their family.

They try eating grass and other adult foods, but they still drink their mother's milk.

By the time they reach five months of age, the young prarie dogs will be fully grown.

a baby prairie dog eating grass

baby prairie dogs playing together

Female prairie dogs stay with their families for their whole lives. Male prairie dogs leave home when they are about two years old.

21

Science Lab

Prairie Dog Escape!

A badger is near a prairie dog town.

The prairie dogs must run to the closest burrow hole and dive underground!

Look at the picture and try answering these questions:

- **Which hole should Prairie Dog A run to?**
- **Which hole do you think is closest to Prairie Dog B?**
- **Should Prairie Dog C run to Hole 3 or Hole 4?**

To help you answer these questions, use a ruler or a piece of string to measure the distances between the prairie dogs and the holes.

- **Were your estimates correct?**

(The answer to this activity is on page 24.)

badger

hole

A

1

2

3

4

B

C

Science Words

burrow (BUR-oh) a hole or tunnel that is dug by an animal to live in

mate (MAYT) to come together in order to have young

prairies (PRAIR-eez) large areas of flat land covered with grass

predators (PRED-uh-turz) animals that hunt and eat other animals for food

squirrel (SKWUR-uhl) an animal with a bushy tail that lives in burrows or trees

territory (TER-uh-*tor*-ee) the area where an animal lives and finds its food

Index

Read More

George, Lynn. *Prairie Dogs: Tunnel Diggers (Animal Architects)*. New York: PowerKids Press (2011).

Markle, Sandra. *Prairie Dogs (Animal Prey)*. Minneapolis, MN: Lerner (2007).

Learn More Online

To learn more about prairie dogs, visit
www.bearportpublishing.com/TheHoleTruth!

Answers

Answers to the activity on page 22
• Prairie Dog A should run to Hole 2.
• Hole 4 is closest to Prairie Dog B.
• Prairie Dog C should run to Hole 3.

About the Author

Dee Phillips lives near the ocean on the southwest coast of England. She writes nonfiction and fiction books for children. Dee's biggest ambition is to one day walk the entire coast of Britain—it will take about ten months!